Diet recommendations for TCM - Liver - Gallbladder Qi-deficiency

Please check these recommendations always with a TCM nutrition consultant, therapist, doctor or dietician. The recipes and the list of ingredients are supporting also the conventional medical therapy. The calorie disclosures of fresh ingredients (fruit and vegetables) vary according to quality and time of harvest. The contents were checked by a dietician and a nutrition consultant for the Traditional Chinese Medicine (TCM).

Author:
©2017 Josef Miligui
www.ebns.at

Source:
The lists are created from the EBNS database for nutritional counseling. The database is used by dietitians, therapists and doctors for advising the patient / client.

Literature:
The specialist literature and the training documents of the German and Austrian dietary and traditional Chinese medicine serve as a knowledge base. We have used the documents as a basis of knowledge, adapted it to our experience and completed them.
http://di-book.com

Title Photo:
©2008 Erika Weixlbaumer

Production and publishing:
BoD – Books on Demand, Norderstedt
ISBN: 9783752862331

Diet recommendations for TCM - Liver - Gallbladder Qi-deficiency

1 Treatment strategy

Strengthen gallbladder and warm it up.

2 Avoid

n.a.

3 Breakfast

	kkal. per serving
Adzuki Bean and Rice Soup	199
Apple sauce with raisins	73
Barley soup	265
Carrot and rice gruel soup	101
Compote from apples	67
Compote from blueberries	49
Corn coffee with cardamom	3
Couscous Salad	338

4 Snack

5 Lunch

6 Afternoon

7 Dinner

8 Any time

9 Recipes

(recommendable) = You can use more.
(little) = You should use less than specified or omit.

9.1 8 treasures of rice

Strengthens kidney and bladder, builds up Qi, strengthens the spleen, repels moisture, reduces internal heat, prevents cancer, builds heart, calms nerves.
Cooking time approx. 1 hour
Calories p. portion: 212
4 portions

Quantity of ingredients
Lily bulbs 1 table spoon / 5g. (recommended)...................................*
Longane 1 table spoon / 5g. (yes) ....*
King Solomon's-seal 1 table spoon / 5g. (recommended)..................*
Yam root, yam root tuber 1 table spoon / 5g. (recommended)...........*
Coix (seeds) YiYi Ren 1 table spoon / 5g. (recommended) ....*
Rice wild (nature rice) 1 1/2 cups / 240g. (little)..........................metal
Water 8-10 cups / 800g. (yes) .... earth

Cooking instructions:
Each one 1 tbsp: Bai He, Longan, Yu Zhu, Da Zao, Shan Yao, Lian Mi, Yi Yi Ren, Qian Shi
Add hot water and soak for about 30 minutes. Then add 1 - 2 cups of rice (normal) and simmer for 1/2 to 1 hour until the rice is very soft. Or: Cook for about 3 hours with the herbs a congee. Then the herbs do not have to be soaked.

9.2 Adzuki Bean and Rice Soup

Reduces moisture, directs down, reduces gastrointestinal heat, builds up essence, strengthens muscles after heat illness, builds up body fluids.
Cooking time approx. 2 hours
Calories p. portion: 199
1 portions

Quantity of ingredients
Adzuki beans 8 table spoons / 40g. (recommended).................water
Rice round grain 2 table spoons / 20g. (yes)...........................metal
Water 1 1/2 cups / 200g. (yes)... earth
Honey 1 table spoon / 8g. (recommended) .... earth

Cooking instructions:
Boil soaked adzuki beans and round grain rice in a ratio of 4: 1 in water
until a thin pulb has formed. Sweet as needed; possibly puree.
Effect: This recipe strengthens kidney, spleen and stomach and is
particularly suitable for mothers with too little milk flow.

9.3   Antipasti

Cools and moves blood, reduces external and internal wind, reduces
internal heat, cools heat, reduces mucus, relaxes, distributes, nourishes
liver-Yin.
Cooking time approx. 40 min
Calories p. portion: 100
3 portions

Quantity of ingredients
Pepperoni 1 piece / 5g. (little)... fire
Lemon juice 1 table spoon / 10g. (yes) ....wood
Aubergine 1 piece / 300g. (recommended) .... earth
Tomato 4 pieces / 200g. (recommended) ....wood
Zucchini 5/8 oz / 200g. (recommended)..................................... earth
Lemon peel 1/2 piece / 3g. (yes).. fire
Olive oil 1 table spoon / 15g. (recommended)........................... earth
Basil (fresh) 8 leaves / 5g. (recommended)..............................metal
Salt 1 pinch / 0,5g. (little)..water
Coriander 1/2 teaspoon / 2g. (recommended)...........................metal

Cooking instructions:
Preheat the oven to 250 degrees Celsius and bake the hot peppers until
the bowl becomes dark (about 20 minutes). Cover the hot peppers with
a clear film and allow to cool. Peel the skin and cut into strips about 2
cm wide. Cut tomatoes in half and spread with oil in slices of aubergine
and bake in the oven at 200 degrees golden brown (about 10 minutes)
Fry the zucchini slices in the grill pan (without fat).
Mix everything together, mix the marinade of olive oil, salt and lemon
peel and pour over the vegetables, sprinkle with coriander. Leave for 1
hour.

9.4   Apple sauce with raisins

Nourishes fluids, reduces stomach heat, strengthens spleen,
harmonizes stomach, moisturizes, relaxes, builds up Qi.
Cooking time approx. 25 min
Calories p. portion: 74
10 portions
Allergens: O

Quantity of ingredients
Apple (sweet) 2,2 lbs / 1000g. (recommended)........................... earth
Water 1/2 cup / 100g. (yes) .... earth
Raisins 1/8 lbs - 2oz / 50g. (recommended).............................. earth

Cooking instructions:
Wash, peel and quarter the apples and remove the core. Put the apples
with the water in a pot. Wash the raisins with hot water and add them.
Cook at low heat for about 10 minutes, then allow to cool. For children
up to 10 months, mash in the blender finely. For the larger ones, crush
with the potato steamer. Fill and seal in a freezer or empty yoghurt jug.
Close the yoghurt jug. Freeze in the shock freezer.
If necessary, thaw at room temperature for about 6 hours. (Lasting
about 4 months).
The fruit mousse is intended as dessert or intermediate meal. It has an
anti-digestive effect. In case of diarrhea give better banana.

9.5   Barley soup

Works neutral to slightly warming and relaxes the Qi flow. Helps with
loss of appetite and diarrhea due to spleen weakness. With weak
spleen qi, one should often eat salty soups for breakfast.
Cooking time approx. 25 min
Calories p. portion: 265
2 portions
Allergens: A

Quantity of ingredients
Barley 1 cup / 120g. (yes)... earth
Salt 1 pinch / 1g. (little)..water
Ginger fresh 1/2 teaspoon / 1g. (recommended)........................metal
Olive oil 1 table spoon / 10g. (recommended)............................ earth
Parsley 2 table spoons / 30g. (recommended)........................... wood
Water 1 1/2 cups / 240g. (yes)... earth

Cooking instructions:
Roast the barley in the pan, then grind it to the ground, and boil with water, some salt and ginger to a mash. Before serving add oil and parsley.

Variant: You can add a better taste to the dish if you cook it with prepared vegetable or meat broth.

9.6 Basic recipe for a beef broth (clear)

Strengthens Qi and Yang, is very warming.
Cooking time approx. 4-8 hours
Calories p. portion: 114
10 portions
Allergens: O

Quantity of ingredients
Beef soup meat 1,1 lbs / 500g. .... earth
Beef meatbones 5/8 oz / 200g. .... earth
Vinegar (Red wine vinegar) 1 dash / 3g. .... wood
Juniper berry 8 pieces / 6g. .... fire
Rosemary 1 pinch / 1g. .... fire
Carrot 3 pieces / 210g. .... earth
Parsnip 2 pieces / 300g. .... fire
Leek 1 piece / 200g. ....metal
Ginger fresh 1/2 teaspoon / 5g. ....metal
Lovage 1 stem / 15g. ....metal
Clove 2 pieces / 2g. ....metal
Pimento 6 pieces / 12g. ....metal
Anise (Common Fennel) 2 pieces / 1g. .... earth
Salt 1 teaspoon / 5g. ....water
Water 3,3 lbs / 1300g. .... earth

Cooking instructions:
Heat water, a dash of red wine vinegar, some juniper berries, a little rosemary, bones and meat till it boils; add carrot, parsnip, leek, ginger, lovage, clove, allspice, star anise and a little salt; simmer for 4-8 hours then strain.
Refrigerate for later use.

9.7 Basic recipe for a chicken broth worming

Strengthens Qi and blood, is very warm.
Cooking time approx. 2-3 hours
Calories p. portion: 90
9 portions
Allergens: L

Quantity of ingredients

Chicken meat 1/2 piece / 600g. ....wood
Carrot 2 pieces / 150g. .... earth
Leek 1 stick / 45g. ....metal
Celery root 1 piece / 500g. .... earth
Ginger fresh 2 slices / 2g. ....metal
Fenugreek (Trigonella foenum-graecum) 1 teaspoon / 2g. ....*
Juniper berry 1 teaspoon / 3g. .... fire
Bay leaf 3 pieces / 2g. ....*
Water 4 cup / 900g. .... earth

Cooking instructions:

Remove chicken parts from fat. Place chicken pieces in a saucepan
with hot water and heat till it boils briefly, skimming any resulting foam.
Add coarsely chopped vegetables and all spices and cook over medium
heat for 2 to 3 hours. Strain the finished soup. Throw away vegetables
and bones.
Tip: If you want to use the meat as a soup insert, take out after 45
minutes and return only the bones in the soup.
Refrigerate for later use.

9.8 Basic recipe for a duck broth

Forces Qi, strengthens blood and fluids, nourishes Yin, forces stomach,
cools heat, strengthens spleen and liver.
Cooking time approx. 2-3 hours
Calories p. portion: 61
6 portions
Allergens: L

Quantity of ingredients

Duck (heart) 5/8 oz / 200g. ....wood
Water 2 cup / 450g. .... earth
Duck (slaughtered) 1/4 lbs - 4oz / 100g. ....wood
Carrot 2 pieces / 100g. .... earth
Celery root 1/2 piece / 600g. .... earth

Cooking instructions:
Cook duck pieces with vegetables for 2-3 hours. Sift broth through a fine sieve and refrigerate for later use.

The innards can be reused: You cut them finely and leaves them for a few minutes with fresh vegetables in the broth draw. Sprinkle with parsley before serving.

9.9 Basic recipe for a fish broth

Strengthens kidney Qi and Yin, strengthens blood and fluids, promotes urination.
Cooking time approx. 40 min
Calories p. portion: 128
5 portions
Allergens: DLO

Quantity of ingredients
Fish pieces mixed (fresh water) 3/4 lbs / 300g. ....water
Celery root 1/4 lbs - 4oz / 120g. .... earth
Leek 2 inches / 10g. ....metal
Carrot 2 pieces / 150g. .... earth
White wine 1/2 cup / 125g. ....wood
Lemon 1/2 piece / 50g. ....wood
Bay leaf 2 leaves / 2g. ....*
Peppercorns 3 pieces / 2g. ....metal
Olive oil 1 table spoon / 10g. .... earth
Water 2 cup / 450g. .... earth

Cooking instructions:
Fry celery, chopped carrots and leeks in olive oil, add bay leaf and peppercorns, add pieces of fish and sauté briefly. Add water, add little white wine or lemon. Simmer gently for 30 minutes. Skim off the resulting foam several times. In the end, sift the ingredients through a cloth.
Refrigerate for later use.

9.10 Basic recipe for a reissue soup (Congee)

Warms the stomach and spleen, harmonizes the intestine, forces Qi,
reduces moisture.
Cooking time approx. 2-4 hours
Calories p. portion: 140
3 portions
Allergens:

Quantity of ingredients
Rice variety any 1 cup / 120g. ....metal
Water 6 cups / 700g. .... earth

Cooking instructions:
Cook rice and water in a ratio of about 1: 6. The amount of water
determines the thickness of the mash (matter of taste).
Put the rice in a saucepan with a heavy lid. It is important to simmer the
rice after a short boil on the slightest flame, otherwise it burns.
Boil the rice for 2-4 hours. The longer he cooks, the more he
strengthens.
If you want to eat the dish for breakfast, you can put the rice on just
before bedtime.
To be on the safe side, you should first check the behavior of your pot
and cooker under observation for a similar amount of time, so that
nothing burns.
Refrigerate for later use.

9.11 Basic recipe for a vegetable soup, nutritious

Strengthens spleen and lung, regulates Qi flow, builds up Qi, dries out,
passes downwardly, strengthens stomach Qi.
Cooking time approx. 2-3 hours
Calories p. portion: 48
5 portions
Allergens: L

Quantity of ingredients
Olive oil 1 table spoon / 4g. .... earth
Onion white 1 piece / 60g. ....metal
Carrot 3 pieces / 200g. .... earth
Parsnip 3/8 lbs - 6oz / 150g. .... fire

Celery root 1 cup / 100g. .... earth
Ginger fresh 1/2 teaspoon / 2g. ....metal
Lemon 1/2 piece / 25g. ....wood
Juniper berry 6 pieces / 6g. .... fire
Thyme dried 1 pinch / 1g. ....metal
Lovage 1 table spoon / 3g. ....metal
Bay leaf 2 leaves / 1g. ....*
Salt 1 pinch / 1g. ....water
Water 3 cups / 650g. .... earth

Cooking instructions:
Cut the vegetables into cubes.
Heat oil in hot pot, fry shortly onions and vegetables.
Add cold water, then add ginger, bay leaf and lemon juice.
Season with juniper, thyme and lovage. Cover for 2 - 3 hours on a low heat and simmer.
The used vegetables should be thrown away.
The basic recipe serves as a soup base and to refine vegetables, legumes or cereals.
If you want to eat vegetable soup immediately, add the desired vegetables half an hour before.
Refrigerate for later use.

9.12 Basmati rice + Zucchini tofu dish

Converts mucus, reduces heat, builds up Qi, nourishes fluids, harmonizes spleen and stomach, forces Lungen Qi.
Cooking time approx. 20 min
Calories p. portion: 146
4 portions
Allergens: E

Quantity of ingredients
Soy Tofu 5/8 lbs - 8oz / 250g. (little) .... earth
Olive oil 2 table spoons / 6g. (recommended)... earth
Coriander 1/2 teaspoon / 4g. (recommended)..metal
Ginger fresh 1/2 teaspoon / 4g. (recommended)..metal
Rice Basmati 1/2 cup / 60g. (yes)..metal
Water 3 cups / 200g. (yes) .... earth
Zucchini 1 piece / 700g. (recommended)... earth

Cooking instructions:
Cut tofu cubes and marinate with olive oil, tamari, crushed coriander and ginger. Leave at least 1 hour.

Cook Basmati rice with the water. You can season with onion and cardamom.
Roast zucchini and tofu in pan in the hot oil for approx. 5-7 min.
Serve rice and tofu on a plate.
Add the parsley.

Can also be used as a salad for the home and on the go.

9.13 Black root with yogurt

Nourishes Yin, relaxes, builds up Qi, moisturises dryness, preserves the fluids.
Cooking time approx. 20 min
Calories p. portion: 424
2 portions
Allergens: AG

Quantity of ingredients
Salsify 1 lbs / 400g. (recommended)... earth
Yogurt (natural, 1.5% fat) 4 table spoons / 80g. (recommended)... fire
Herbs various 1 table spoon / 8g. (yes) ....*
Salt 1 pinch / 1g. (little)...water
Herbs various 2 table spoons / 6g. (yes)...*
Multi-grain bread (gray bread) 6 slices / 120g. (little).................. wood

Cooking instructions:
Peel the salsify and simmer in salted water until tender. Pour away the water, cool the salsify and cut it to size. Cover with yoghurt and sprinkle with fresh herbs. Serve with the bread.
You can also use the salsify from the conserve.

9.14 Black-eyed beans stew

Strengthens spleen and kidney, is very nutritious, warms the stomach and spleen, harmonizes the intestine, forces Qi, strengthens stomach and kidney, strengthens spleen and kidney.
Cooking time approx. 20 min
Calories p. portion: 140
5 portions

Quantity of ingredients
Black-eyed peas 1 cup / 100g. (recommended)........................water
Rice variety any 1 1/2 cups / 200g. (yes) ....metal
Water 10 cups / 1000g. (yes).. earth

Cooking instructions:
Soak the beans overnight and strain.

In a ratio of 1: 2, simmer the beans together with the rice in the Water.
Depending on how hot the flame is and how thin the dish should be,
more water must be added.

Variation: Add vegetables fried in oil, such as carrots, celery tubers,
onions or leeks.

9.15 Carrot and rice gruel soup

Warms the stomach and spleen, harmonizes the intestine, forces Qi,
reduces moisture, strengthens spleen and liver, regulates Qi flow,
moisturizes, relaxes, builds up Qi, spreads.
Cooking time approx. 10 min
Calories p. portion: 101
1 portions

Quantity of ingredients
Basic recipe for a rice soup (Congee) 1 cup / 120g. (recommended) *
Carrot 2 pieces / 100g. (recommended).................................... earth
Salt 1 teaspoon / 4g. (little)..water

Cooking instructions:
Peel and grate carrots. Heat the rice soup (according to the basic
recipe) till it boils and add the grated carrots and salt. Cook for 10
minutes.

9.16 Celery and tomato salad

Nourishes liver-Yin, produces humors, brings the liver Qi in motion,
cools heat, relaxes, builds up Qi.
Cooking time approx. 10 min
Calories p. portion: 245
1 portions
Allergens: GHL

Quantity of ingredients

Celery sticks 3-4 twigs / 50g. (recommended) .... earth
Tomato 4 pieces / 200g. (recommended) .... wood
Basil 3 leaves (fresh) / 1g. (recommended)................................metal
Yogurt (natural, 1.5% fat) 2 table spoons / 30g. (recommended)... fire
Olive oil 1/2 teaspoon / 5g. (recommended).............................. earth
Lemon juice 1 table spoon / 10g. (yes) .... wood
Salt 1 pinch / 0,5g. (little)..water
Sugar white 1 pinch / 0,5g. (little).. earth
Pepper (ground) 1 pinch / 0,2g. (yes) ....metal
Hazelnuts 2 table spoons / 20g. (little)...................................... earth

Cooking instructions:
Clean celery, possibly remove threads and cut into fine rings. Wash
tomatoes and dice. For the sauce, mix yoghurt with olive oil and lemon
juice and season with the spices. Add the prepared tomatoes and
celery to the sauce and mix. Finely chop whole hazelnuts or sprinkle
ground hazelnuts over the fresh food and serve the salad garnished
with basil leaves.

9.17 Celery salad with lemon and olive oil

Strengthens stomach Qi, moisturizes, relaxes, builds up Qi.
Cooking time approx. 10 min
Calories p. portion: 402
1 portions
Allergens: L

Quantity of ingredients

Celery root 1/2 piece / 200g. (recommended) .... earth
Lemon juice 1/2 piece / 10g. (yes) .... wood
Olive oil 4 table spoons / 40g. (recommended) .... earth

Cooking instructions:
Peel celeriac and cut into pieces and rub. Serve with the lemon juice
and olive oil.

9.18 Chicken soup with angelica root and buckthorn fruit

Strengthens spleen and nourishes the blood and Yin of the liver, forces Qi and blood, is very warming.
Cooking time approx. 1 1/2 hours
Calories p. portion: 77
3 portions
Allergens: LO

Quantity of ingredients
Basic recipe for a chicken soup 2 cup / 500g. (recommended) .... *
Angelica root 1/8 oz / 5g. (recommended) .... *
Bocksdorn fruits, goji berry dried 1/8 lbs - 2oz / 50g. (yes) .... wood

Cooking instructions:
When you cook chicken broth according to basic recipes add angelica root and Bocksdorn fruits in the last 40 minutes.

Ingestion: Drink 2-3 cups of broth daily.

9.19 Chicken soup with egg yolk and parsley

Forces Qi and blood, is very warming, nourishes blood and liver, harmonizes liver and spleen, forces eyesight, preserves the fluids, contracts.
Cooking time approx. 10 min
Calories p. portion: 118
2 portions
Allergens: CL

Quantity of ingredients
Basic recipe for a chicken soup 2 cup / 500g. (recommended) .... *
Chicken yolk 1 piece / 10g. (little) .... earth
Parsley 1 table spoon / 10g. (recommended)............................ wood

Cooking instructions:
Cook the chicken broth according to the basic recipe.
Heat broth and bubble the egg yolk. Sprinkle the chopped parsley over it and let it rest for about 2 minutes. Drink in small sips.

9.20 Chicken soup with green spelt, parsley and sake

Forces Qi and blood, is very warming, nourishes liver-blood, preserves the fluids, contracts, scatters and move Qi, moisturizes, reduces cold-evil, softens knots.
Cooking time approx. 1 1/2 hours
Calories p. portion: 150
2 portions
Allergens: AL

Quantity of ingredients
Basic recipe for a chicken soup 2 cup / 500g. (recommended) ....*
Green spelt 4 table spoons / 30g. (recommended) ....wood
Parsley 2 table spoons / 14g. (recommended)...........................wood
Sake 1 dash / 2g. (little)..metal

Cooking instructions:
Cook the chicken broth according to the basic recipe. Add the ingredients in the soup and simmer 10 min.

9.21 Compote from apples

Nourishes fluids, reduces stomach heat, forces spleen, produces essence, harmonizes stomach, warms the stomach and spleen, promotes blood circulation and conduction flow, relieves cold-sickness and pain.
Cooking time approx. 10 min
Calories p. portion: 67
2 portions

Quantity of ingredients
Apple (sweet) 1 piece / 220g. (recommended)........................... earth
Water 1 1/2 cups / 220g. (yes)... earth
Cinnamon ground 1 pinch / 1g. (recommended) ....*

Cooking instructions:
Cook the apples (organic) with the skin and seeds. Sprinkle with cinnamon.

9.22 Compote from blueberries

Keeps fluids and essence, forces liver and kidneys, forces blood, forces eyesight, reduces internal heat, produces humors, leads Qi down.
Cooking time approx. 10 min
Calories p. portion: 49
1 portions

Quantity of ingredients
Blueberry 1/4 lbs - 4oz / 100g. (recommended) .... wood
Water 1 cup / 120g. (yes) .... earth
Cinnamon ground 1 pinch / 0,1g. (recommended) .... *
Lemon peel 1 pinch / 1g. (yes) .... fire
Sugar cane sugar 1 teaspoon / 3g. (yes) .... earth

Cooking instructions:
Cook the blueberries gently and sprinkle with sugar, cinnamon and grated lemon zest.

9.23 Corn coffee with cardamom

Dries out, passes downwardly.
Cooking time approx. 5 min
Calories p. portion: 3
1 portions

Quantity of ingredients
Cereal coffee 1 table spoon / 15g. (yes) .... fire
Cardamom 2 cores / 1g. (recommended) .... *
Water 1 cup / 120g. (yes) .... earth

Cooking instructions:
Boil water, coffee, sugar and cardamom. Let it set for one min before drinking.

9.24 Couscous Salad

Preserves the fluids, nourishes blood and liver, harmonizes liver, forces eyesight, preserves the fluids.
Cooking time approx. 25 min
Calories p. portion: 338
3 portions
Allergens: A

Quantity of ingredients

Water 1 cup / 100g. (yes)... earth
Olive oil 1 table spoon / 15g. (recommended)............................ earth
Couscous 5/8 oz / 200g. (yes)..wood
Lemon juice 2 table spoons / 30g. (yes)....................................wood
Lemon peel 1 teaspoon / 2g. (yes) .... fire
Tomato 2 pieces / 80g. (recommended) ....wood
Cucumber 1/4 lbs - 4oz / 100g. (little) .... earth
Carrot 1/4 lbs - 4oz / 100g. (recommended)............................. earth
Parsley 1 Bunch / 100g. (recommended)...................................wood
Chives 1 Bunch / 100g. (recommended)....................................metal
Peppermint 3 twigs / 30g. (recommended) ....metal

Cooking instructions:

Boil in a small saucepan 250 ml. water with salt and 1 tablespoon olive oil. Add the couscous, take the stove in the front and let it swell covered for 5 minutes. Put the couscous back on the stove and let it simmer for about 2 minutes with gentle stirring. If necessary, add 1 - 3 tbsp of hot water.

Mix the couscous with lemon juice, chopped lemon peel and 1 tbsp oil, season with salt and pepper and leave to set.

Add couscous with tomatoes, cucumber, parsley (all diced), carrots (grated), chives and mint (finely chopped). Season the couscous salad with lemon juice, salt and pepper.

9.25 Cranberry yogurt mix

Moisturises dryness, preserves the fluids, contracts, preserves the fluids, contracts.
Cooking time approx. 5 min
Calories p. portion: 57
2 portions
Allergens: GO

Quantity of ingredients

Yogurt (natural, 1.5% fat) 1/4 lbs - 4oz / 125g. (recommended) .... fire
Cranberry jam 2 table spoons / 20g. (yes) ....wood
Mineral water 1 cup / 250g. (recommended)..............................water

Cooking instructions:

Mix yoghurt, cranberry jam and mineral water until frothy.

9.26 Figs with mozzarella and honey

Moisturizes the lungs and large intestine, reduces mucusfeuer, passes downwardly, strengthens middle heater, reduces internal heat, dissolves stagnation.
Cooking time approx. 10 min
Calories p. portion: 415
1 portions
Allergens: GO

Quantity of ingredients
Fig 4 pieces / 100g. (yes) .... earth
Mozzarella 1 piece / 50g. (yes) .... *
Basil (fresh) 1/2 bunch / 50g. (recommended) .... metal
Honey 2 table spoons / 24g. (recommended) .... earth
Pepper (ground) 1 pinch / 0,1g. (yes) .... metal
Grapeseed oil 1 table spoon / 12g. (little) .... earth
Vinegar Aceto Balsamico white 1 table spoon / 12g. (yes) .... wood

Cooking instructions:
Quarter fresh figs, dice buffalo mozzarella, pluck basil leaves.
Mix a dressing with light balsamic vinegar, grapeseed oil and honey and season to taste.
Place the figs on the edge of the appropriate plate. Spread the mozzarella cubes and season with black pepper. Spread whole or roughly sliced basil leaves over it and moisten with the marinade.
Spiced pizza bread goes perfectly with it.

9.27 Fish soup with rosemary

Strengthens kidney Qi, strengthens blood and fluids, promotes urination, regulates Qi, dries out, passes downwardly, strengthens spleen and liver, regulates Qi flow, moisturizes, relaxes, builds up Qi, spreads.
Cooking time approx. 30 min
Calories p. portion: 271
4 portions
Allergens: DLO

Quantity of ingredients
Basic recipe for a fish soup 2 cup / 500g. (recommended) .... *
Rosemary 1/2 bunch / 7g. (yes) .... fire
Onion (spring onion) 1 piece / 20g. (little) .... metal
Olive oil 2 table spoons / 35g. (recommended) .... earth

Fish pieces mixed (fresh water) 5/8 lbs - 8oz / 250g. (yes).........water
Carrot 1 piece / 120g. (recommended) .... earth
Parsnip 1 piece / 180g. (recommended) .... fire
Celery root 1 slice / 20g. (recommended) .... earth
Salt 1 pinch / 1g. (little)...water
Peppercorns 2 pieces / 1g. (yes)..metal
Garlic 1 clove / 3g. (recommended)..metal

Cooking instructions:
Fry the onion and garlic in oil. Add fish broth. Add diced carrots, parsnips and celery. Season with salt and peppercorns. Simmer the soup on a low heat for 25 minutes.
Wash the fish, drizzle with lemon juice, divide into pieces and add to the soup with the pink rosemary. Cook for 5 min on low heat.
Add the chives and parsley and season the soup with the salt.

9.28 Fruit jelly

Cools heat, nourishes fluids, produces humors, leads Qi down, warms the stomach and spleen, promotes blood circulation and conduction flow.
Cooking time approx. 2 hours and more
Calories p. portion: 60
2 portions

Quantity of ingredients
Carrot (Early Carrot) 3/4 lbs / 300g. (recommended) .... earth
Water 6 table spoons / 50g. (yes).. earth
Sugar cane sugar 1 teaspoon / 3g. (yes)................................... earth
Gelatin white 1 Leaf / 3g. (recommended) .... *
Orange 1/2 piece / 50g. (yes) .... wood
Cinnamon ground 1 pinch / 0,2g. (recommended) .... *
Corn germ oil 1/2 teaspoon / 2g. (little) .... earth

Cooking instructions:
Thoroughly wash, clean, peel and slice the carrots.
Boil about 6 tablespoons of water in a saucepan, add the carrots and cane sugar and cook over medium heat for 10-15 minutes.
Meanwhile, soak the gelatin in cold water for about 10 minutes.
Squeeze the orange half, mix the juice with the cinnamon and the oil.
Crush the hot carrots with the blender and dissolve the gelatine (alternative: use agar-agar) in the hot mush.
Stir in the orange juice. Swirl out a pudding mold (1/4 liter content) with

cold water, pour in the carrot sauce and refrigerate in the fridge for about 3 hours.
Tip out before eating and allow to warm to room temperature.

9.29 Fruit juice

Nourishes fluids, reduces stomach heat, produces essence, harmonizes stomach, strengthens spleen and liver, regulates Qi flow, moisturizes, relaxes, builds up Qi, spreads, cools heat, nourishes fluids, moisturizes lungs, strengthens middle heater, moisturizes.
Cooking time approx. 10 min
Calories p. portion: 176
2 portions

Quantity of ingredients
Orange 2 pieces / 150g. (yes) .... wood
Apple (sweet) 4 pieces / 300g. (recommended) .... earth
Carrot 2 pieces / 150g. (recommended) .... earth
Honey 1 table spoon / 10g. (recommended) .... earth

Cooking instructions:
Peel oranges and carrots. Cut all ingredients into cubes so that they fit into the juicer and juice. Sweet with honey.

9.30 Grated apple

Preserves the fluids, contracts.
Cooking time approx. 10 min
Calories p. portion: 120
1 portions

Quantity of ingredients
Apple (sour) 1 piece / 200g. (recommended) .... wood

Cooking instructions:
Peel apple and grate as fine as possible. Leave for at least 5 minutes until it turns brown.

9.31 Grated carrots with apple

Strengthens spleen and liver, regulates Qi flow, moisturizes, relaxes, builds up Qi, spreads, nourishes fluids, reduces stomach heat, forces spleen, produces essence, harmonizes stomach, cools heat, preserves the fluids, contracts.
Cooking time approx. 10 min
Calories p. portion: 74
1 portions

Quantity of ingredients
Carrot 1/4 lbs - 4oz / 100g. (recommended).............................. earth
Apple (sweet) 1 piece / 50g. (recommended)............................ earth
Lemon juice 2 teaspoons / 3g. (yes)..wood
Sugar substitute (sweetener) 1g. Or 0,034oz / 1g. (recommended)...*

Cooking instructions:
Mix lemon juice with sweetener. Grate the washed, thinly peeled carrots and the apple piece into the sauce and mix.

9.32 Grilled tomatoes with cheese filling

Nourishes liver-Yin, cools heat, produces humors, gets Qi moving, reduces internal heat, dries out, passes downwardly, preserves the fluids.
Cooking time approx. 30 min
Calories p. portion: 470
2 portions
Allergens: ACG

Quantity of ingredients
Tomato 8 pieces / 200g. (recommended) ....wood
Feta cheese 0,2 lbs / 75g. (little).. fire
Fresh cheese 0,2 lbs / 75g. (little)...wood
Chicken egg 1 piece / 60g. (yes) .... earth
Olive oil 1 table spoon / 12g. (recommended)............................ earth
Basil (fresh) 1 table spoon / 6g. (recommended).......................metal
Salt 1 pinch / 1g. (little)...water
Pepper (ground) 1 pinch / 0,5g. (yes) ....metal
Olives 1 oz / 30g. (little)... fire
Rucola 1/4 lbs / 100g. (recommended) .... fire
White bread (wheat bread) 4 slices / 80g. (yes).........................wood

Cooking instructions:
Hollow out tomatoes generously. Put in a casserole dish.
Mix cheese, olive oil, egg, chopped basil and flour. Season with salt and pepper and fill in the tomatoes.
Bake in the preheated oven at 210 degrees on the middle rail for 15 minutes, then switch on the oven grill and grill for a further 3 minutes (without circulating air).
Stone the olives and chop and sprinkle on the tomatoes.
Garnish tomatoes with rocket and serve with white bread.

9.33 Halibut with tomato and garlic sauce

Nourishes liver-Yin, cools heat, produces humors, warms the stomach and spleen, harmonizes the intestine, forces Qi, reduces moisture, reduces internal heat, reduces mucus, produces humors, dries out, passes downwardly.
Cooking time approx. 45 min
Calories p. portion: 319
5 portions
Allergens: D

Quantity of ingredients
Rice variety any 1 cup / 120g. (yes)..metal
Water 6 cups / 240g. (yes) .... earth
Salt 1 pinch / 1g. (little)...water
Halibut (Flatfish) 2,2 lbs / 800g. (yes) ....water
Salt 1 pinch / 1g. (little)...water
Pepper (ground) 1 pinch / 0,5g. (yes) ....metal
Lemon juice 1 dash / 2g. (yes)..wood
Bay leaf 2 pieces / 2g. (recommended) ....*
Lemon 1 piece / 30g. (yes)..wood
Garlic 8 pieces / 10g. (recommended).......................................metal
Thyme dried 1 table spoon / 5g. (recommended).......................metal
Olives 0,2 lbs / 75g. (little) .... fire
Tomato 4 pieces / 200g. (recommended) ....wood
Salt 1 pinch / 1g. (little)...water
Pepper (ground) 1 pinch / 0,5g. (yes) ....metal

Cooking instructions:
Cook rice with salted water (1:3).
Rinse the fish under running cold water, dab with kitchen paper and rub with salt, pepper and lemon juice.
Place the fish fillets in a casserole dish with pieces of bay leaf.

Wash the lemon hot and cut into slices, peel and halve the garlic.
Sprinkle the olives and the thyme over them.
Brew the tomatoes with hot water, skin and chop.

Mix all ingredients, season with salt and pepper and distribute around the fish.

Cook everything at 200°C/392°F for about 20 minutes.
Serve with the rice.

9.34 Kudzu soup in the morning

Moisturizes, relaxes, builds up Qi, spreads, forces stomach, harmonizes middle, reduces internal heat, detoxifies, softens, passes downwardly.
Cooking time approx. 5 min
Calories p. portion: 12
1 portions
Allergens: E

Quantity of ingredients
Water 1 cup / 250g. (yes) .... earth
Soy sauce 1 dash / 2g. (yes) ....water
Umeboshi paste 1 knife tip / 2g. (yes)...water

Cooking instructions:
Mix kudzu with cold water and heat till it boils while stirring. Once it is glassy, remove from heat and let cool. Season with Tamari and Umeboshipaste or crushed umeboshi plums

There is always the possibility to support your stomach and intestines with this recipe, taken before the right breakfast.
A morning cure for stomach and mucous membranes. Fix the base balance.

9.35 Legumes

Strengthens spleen and liver, regulates Qi flow, moisturizes, relaxes, builds up Qi, spreads, nourishes blood and Qi, diuretic, harmonizes Qi (in the middle and lower heater), detoxifies, reduces internal heat and moisture.
Cooking time approx. 30 min
Calories p. portion: 31
5 portions

Quantity of ingredients

Pinto beans speckled 1/4 lbs - 4oz / 100g. (recommended) ....water
Lentils 1/8 lbs - 2oz / 50g. (little)...water
Peas, green 1/8 lbs - 2oz / 50g. (recommended) ....water
Water 4 cup / 1000g. (yes)... earth
Lemon 1 slice / 2g. (yes).. wood
Juniper berry 6 pieces / 2g. (recommended)............................... fire
Thyme 1 Twig / 3g. (recommended) .... *
Rosemary 1 Twig / 3g. (yes)... fire
Carrot 1 piece / 100g. (recommended) .... earth
Savory 1-2 teaspoons / 5g. (recommended) ....water
Ginger fresh a great piece / 3g. (recommended).......................metal
Bay leaf 2-3 leaves / 1g. (recommended) .... *
Wakame 1-2 strips / 1g. (recommended) ....water

Cooking instructions:

Legumes such as beans, lentils, peas or chickpeas are soaked in plenty
of cold water for several hours to three days. The water should be
changed every 8 hours. Then pour off soaking water and wash legumes
thoroughly.

Preparation:
Cook the legumes with fresh cold water and a slice of ginger and bring
to froth. Cook without lid for about 5 minutes, scooping off the foam.
Only then add the following ingredients: a slice of lemon or lemon juice,
crush juniper berries, thyme; (possibly 1 knife tip of asafoetida in case
of severe indigestion). Add savory, sage, juniper, fenugreek seeds,
carrots, bay leaves, fresh ginger, wakame algae.
Simmer on the slightest flame until beans or lentils have the desired
consistency.
This base can be stored for 3-4 days in the refrigerator.

9.36 Lentils and rice stew

Strengthens spleen and liver, regulates Qi flow, moisturizes, relaxes,
builds up Qi, spreads, warms the stomach and spleen, harmonizes the
intestine, forces Qi, reduces moisture, brings the liver Qi in motion,
cools heat.
Cooking time approx. 25 min
Calories p. portion: 232
3 portions
Allergens: LNO

Quantity of ingredients
Lentils 1/4 lbs - 4oz / 100g. (little) .... water
Water 5 cups / 500g. (yes) .... earth
Rice variety any 1 cup / 120g. (yes)... metal
Sesame oil 1 table spoon / 10g. (little)..................................... earth
Carrot 2 pieces / 150g. (recommended).................................... earth
Celery sticks 2 rods / 20g. (recommended).............................. earth
Cumin (Caraway seed) 1 pinch / 0,2g. (recommended) .... metal
Salt 1 pinch / 0,5g. (little)... water
Vinegar (Apple vinegar) 1 dash / 2g. (recommended)................ wood
Parsley 2 table spoons / 18g. (recommended)........................... wood

Cooking instructions:
Soak the dry lentils the day before.
Heat sesame oil in a hot pot; cut carrot and celery into small pieces and
sauté; add rice, a pinch of cumin and lentils
 and heat till it boils.
If the lenses are soft, add salt; season with a little vinegar and garnish
with parsley.

Variant: In summer you can omit the cumin and add fresh green peas,
Chinese cabbage or celery.

9.37 Melanzani with olive oil and turmeric

Cools and moves blood, reduces external and internal wind, reduces
internal heat, nourishes liver-Yin, cools heat, produces humors,
moisturizes, relaxes, builds up Qi, spreads.
Cooking time approx. 30 min
Calories p. portion: 432
2 portions
Allergens: A

Quantity of ingredients
Aubergine 2 pieces / 300g. (recommended) .... earth
Olive oil 4 table spoons / 60g. (recommended).......................... earth
Tomato 4 pieces / 200g. (recommended) .... wood
Turmeric (yellow root) 1/2 teaspoon / 1g. (recommended) .... *
Ground 1 pinch / 1g. (yes)... earth
Salt 1 pinch / 1g. (little)... water
White bread (wheat bread) 4 slices / 80g. (yes)......................... wood

Cooking instructions:
Cut the melanzani into slices and spread them with the tomatoes on a baking tray. Sprinkle with olive oil and then with turmeric, caraway and salt. Bake them in the tube 20 min.
Serve with the white bread.

9.38 Miso soup with tofu

Nourish the humors, preserves the fluids, contracts, nourishes fluids, lets Qi ascend, harmonizes spleen and stomach, moisturizes, relaxes, builds up Qi, spreads, regulates Qi, warms spleen and kidney, dissolves stagnation, directs upwards.
Cooking time approx. 5 min
Calories p. portion: 51
3 portions
Allergens: E

Quantity of ingredients
Wakame 1 piece / 5g. (recommended) .... water
Miso 3-4 table spoons / 30g. (yes).. water
Soy Tofu 1/8 lbs - 2oz / 50g. (little) .... earth
Water 2 cup / 500g. (yes).. earth
Soy sauce 1 dash / 3g. (yes) .... water
Onion (spring onion) 1/2 teaspoon / 6g. (little) .... metal

Cooking instructions:
Boil soybean seedlings, wakame algae and diced tofu for 5 minutes. Put the miso paste in the soup plate and slowly pour over the soup. Season with Tamari sauce. Sprinkle with cutted spring onion.

9.39 Nettle-chard soup

Drains moisture down, strengthens blood, cools liver heat.
Cooking time approx. 30 min
Calories p. portion: 52
4 portions

Quantity of ingredients
Nettles Handful / 10g. (recommended) .... wood
Chard 1 lbs / 500g. (recommended) .... earth
Salt 1 pinch / 1g. (little).. water
Water 2 cup / 400g. (yes).. earth
Olive oil 1 table spoon / 10g. (recommended)........................... earth
Pepper (ground) 1 pinch / 0,5g. (yes) .... metal

Cooking instructions:
Heat the oil in a saucepan, add the washed and finely chopped Swiss chard. Salt and let simmer for 10 minutes. Add the chopped nettles and cook for another 10 minutes. Add pepper and puree.

9.40 Potato-basil soup

Strengthens stomach Qi, moisturizes, relaxes, builds up Qi, spreads, forces Qi, forces spleen, relieves inflammation, spreads, strengthens spleen and liver, regulates Qi flow.
Cooking time approx. 25 min
Calories p. portion: 96
4 portions
Allergens: L

Quantity of ingredients
Water 2 cups / 450g. (yes) .... earth
Potato 4 pieces / 200g. (recommended) .... earth
Carrot 2 pieces / 100g. (recommended)..................................... earth
Celery root 1 piece / 500g. (recommended)............................... earth
Pepper (ground) 1 pinch / 0,5g. (yes) ....metal
Ground 1 pinch / 1g. (yes)... earth
Garlic 1 clove / 3g. (recommended)...metal
Salt 1 pinch / 1g. (little)..water
Lemon 1 teaspoon / 3g. (yes)..wood
Basil (fresh) 1 Bunch / 50g. (recommended).............................metal
Peppers powder 1 pinch / 1g. (yes) ....*
Sugar cane sugar 1 pinch / 1g. (yes) .... earth
Olive oil 1 table spoon / 10g. (recommended)............................ earth

Cooking instructions:
Peeled and chopped 4 medium potatoes in a pot of hot water and 2 chopped medium carrots, a piece of celery root, a pinch of pepper, a pinch of ground cumin, crushed a small clove of garlic, a pinch of salt, 1 teaspoon of lemon juice, simmer until the Vegetables is soft.

Add 1 bunch finely chopped basil into one half of the soup and puree everything; stir in the other half of the basil; with rose paprika, a pinch of whole cane sugar, 1 tablespoon of olive oil or butter, freshly ground pepper, salt to taste.

9.41 Pumpkin curry

Forces lungs and spleen, diuretic, forces Qi, protects liver, warms the stomach and spleen, harmonizes the intestine, forces Qi, reduces moisture, moisturizes, relaxes, builds up Qi, spreads, nourishes blood and liver, harmonizes liver and spleen.
Cooking time approx. 20 min
Calories p. portion: 193
3 portions

Quantity of ingredients
Pumpkin 3/4 lbs / 300g. (recommended) .... earth
Olive oil 2 table spoons / 30g. (recommended) .... earth
Coriander 1 pinch / 1g. (recommended) .... metal
Pepper (ground) 1 pinch / 0,5g. (yes) .... metal
Curry 1 pinch / 1g. (yes) .... metal
Water 1/4 cup / 50g. (yes) .... earth
Salt 1 pinch / 1g. (little) .... water
Parsley 1 table spoon / 7g. (recommended) .... wood
Cardamom 1 pinch / 1g. (recommended) .... *
Turmeric (yellow root) 1 pinch / 1g. (recommended) .... *
Rice (whole grain) 1/2 cup / 60g. (yes) .... metal
Water 3 cups / 300g. (yes) .... earth
Salt 1 pinch / 1g. (little) .... water

Cooking instructions:
Heat olive oil in pan. Steam the pumpkin cut in cubes, season with cilantro, pepper and curry, simmer with a little water, salt with sea salt, add chopped parsley with cardamom and turmeric, simmer on a small fire for about 10 minutes, depending on the pumpkin, the pumpkin should still be firm.
Place the rice in salted water, bring to the boil and let it simmer over low heat for about 15 minutes.

9.42 Pumpkin-yoghurt soup

Moisturizes, relaxes, builds up Qi, spreads, strengthens spleen and liver, regulates Qi flow, moisturises dryness, preserves the fluids, contracts, gets Qi moving, forces fluid production, reduces cold-evil, directs upwards.
Cooking time approx. 15 min
Calories p. portion: 68
4 portions
Allergens: GL

Quantity of ingredients
Basic recipe for a vegetable soup 1 cup / 300g. (recommended) .... *
Hokkaido pumpkin 1,1 lbs / 500g. (recommended) .... earth
Ginger fresh 1/2 teaspoon / 2g. (recommended)....................... metal
Fennel seeds ground 1/2 teaspoon / 1g. (yes).......................... earth
Anise (Common Fennel) 1/4 teaspoon / 1g. (recommended) ..... earth
Yogurt (natural, 1.5% fat) 3/8 lbs - 6oz / 150g. (recommended) .... fire
Peppermint 2 leaves / 1g. (recommended) .... metal
Salt 1 pinch / 1g. (little).. water

Cooking instructions:
Heat the vegetable broth (after the basic recipe) till it boils . Add diced
pumpkin, chopped ginger, crushed fennel seeds and anise. Bring the
soup to the boil and simmer for about 12 minutes until the pumpkin is
soft.
Remove soup from the heat. Puree the soup with the yoghurt with the
blender. Serve soup with finely chopped mint sprinkled.

9.43 Quinoa piquant with avocado

Nourishes Yin from liver, lungs and colon, moisturizes, relaxes, builds
up Qi, spreads, strengthens spleen and liver, regulates Qi flow,
moisturizes, relaxes, builds up Qi, spreads, forces Qi, dries out,
regulates Qi, warms spleen and kidney, dissolves stagnation
Cooking time approx. 20 min
Calories p. portion: 561
2 portions

Quantity of ingredients
Water 1 1/2 cups / 240g. (yes)... earth
Quinoa 1 cup / 100g. (yes) .... fire
Carrot 1 piece shredded / 100g. (recommended)...................... earth
Onion (spring onion) 2 table spoons (chopped) / 12g. (little) ...... metal
Curcuma 1/2 teaspoon / 1g. (recommended).................................... *
Avocado 1 piece soft / 300g. (little)... earth
Salt 1 pinch / 0,5g. (little)... water
Pepper (ground) 1 pinch / 0,2g. (yes) .... metal
Linseed oil 2 teaspoons / 4g. (little) .... earth

Cooking instructions:
Put quinoa in hot water.
Add grated carrot, pepper and salt, finely chopped spring onion and turmeric.
Simmer about 20 minutes, pull from the fire.
Add pre-cut avocado.
Add a dash of oil and sprinkle with fresh parsley and gomasio.

Spices and herbs: turmeric, cardamom, cress, parsley, chives.

Variation: For those who want more hearty, you can also use a sardine from organic fish preserves. If you are the "protein type", this breakfast will hold on for a long time!

9.44 Radish, apple and yogurt fresh food

Nourishes fluids, reduces stomach heat, forces spleen, produces essence, harmonizes stomach. nourishes the lungs and spleen, distributes mucus, dissolves mucus, dissolves stagnation, directs upwards, moisturises dryness, preserves the fluids, contracts.
Cooking time approx. 10 min
Calories p. portion: 77
2 portions
Allergens: G

Quantity of ingredients
Yogurt (natural, 3.5% fat) 5 table spoons / 50g. (recommended)... fire
Lemon juice 1/2 teaspoon / 2g. (yes) .... wood
Salt 1 pinch / 0,5g. (little) .... water
Pepper white (ground) 1 pinch / 0,1g. (yes) .... metal
Radish (white, green, purple-red) 1/4 lbs - 4oz / 100g. (reco.)....metal
Apple (sweet) 1 piece / 150g. (recommended)........................... earth
Parsley 2 table spoons / 18g. (recommended) .... wood

Cooking instructions:
Mix yoghurt with lemon juice, salt and white pepper.

Wash radish and apple, peel and finely grate. Mix with the yoghurt sauce, let it pass briefly. Sprinkle with chopped parsley.

9.45 Red lentils with avocado and radish

Nutritious and moisturizing builds up Qi and fluids, drives sweat, reduces blood fat, stimulates, dissolves stagnation.
Cooking time approx. 20 min
Calories p. portion: 269
3 portions
Allergens: N

Quantity of ingredients

Ginger fresh 2 slices / 2g. (recommended) ....metal
Water 1 1/2 cups / 200g. (yes)... earth
Lentils red 1 cup peeled / 100g. (little) ....water
Wakame 1 inch / 1g. (recommended)......................................water
Salt 1 pinch / 0,5g. (little)..water
Lemon juice 1 dash / 1g. (yes)...wood
Curcuma 1 pinch / 0,3g. (recommended)...*
Avocado 1 piece / 300g. (little) .... earth
Pepper (ground) 1 pinch / 0,2g. (yes) ....metal
Pepper powder (hot) 1 pinch / 0,2g. (recommended) .... fire
Sesame oil 1 dash / 1g. (little) .... earth
Radish (white, green, purple-red) 1 cup / 100g. (reco.) ....metal

Cooking instructions:

Put in a pot with water, some chopped ginger, peeled red lentils, a piece of wakame or a small amount of hijiki and simmer until the lentils are soft. Season with salt, lemon juice and turmeric.

Meanwhile: place half an avocado per serving on one-third of the plate: add ground pepper, a pinch of salt, a little lemon juice, a pinch of sweet pepper and a little sesame oil.

Put the grated radish on the second plate third.

Fill the lentil dish into the last third of the plate.
Variant: Use radish slices instead of radishes.

9.46 Reissue soup with seaweed

Forces Qi and blood, reduces cold, forces spleen, liver and stomach, strengthens blood and Qi, regulates Qi, warms spleen and kidney, dissolves stagnation, directs upwards.
Cooking time approx. 4-5 hours
Calories p. portion: 130
6 portions
Allergens: L

Quantity of ingredients
Beef meatbones 3/4 lbs / 10g. (recommended)........................... earth
Beef soup meat 7/8 lbs / 400g. (yes) .... earth
Parsley 1/4 Bunch / 25g. (recommended)................................. wood
Juniper berry 4 / 2g. (recommended)... fire
Carrot 2 pieces / 180g. (recommended).................................... earth
Celery root 1/4 lbs / 100g. (recommended)............................... earth
Onion (spring onion) 1/2 piece / 10g. (little).............................. metal
Peppercorns 4 / 1g. (yes)... metal
Lovage 1 Twig / 3g. (recommended) .... metal
Wakame 1 inch / 3g. (recommended) .... water
Rice variety any 2 table spoons / 20g. (yes)............................. metal
Water 4 cup / 900g. (yes)... earth

Cooking instructions:
Boil parsley in water. Add the juniper berries, meat bones, a piece of soup, carrot and a piece of celery tuber, a separately tanned onion half, a few peppery grains, a belly and a piece of wakame algae; Allow 4-8 hours to simmer and then strain. Add the rice and simmer for another 1/2 hour.
Keep the stock in the refrigerator.
Variant: If you remove the meat after 1-2 hours, you can still dice it well and use it later as a supporter.

9.47 Rhubarb and apple jelly

Moisturizes, relaxes, builds up Qi, spreads, cools heat, preserves the fluids, contracts, strengthens middle heater, moisturizes, cools heat, distributes mucus, derives wind-cold and wind-heat, brings the stomach Qi in motion, solves congestion.
Cooking time approx. 15 min
Calories p. portion: 180
2 portions

Quantity of ingredients

Rhubarb 5/8 oz / 200g. (recommended) ....wood
Apple juice (natural cloudy) 1 cup / 300g. (yes)......................... earth
Corn starch 1 oz / 30g. (yes) .... earth
Honey 1/2 oz / 20g. (recommended)... earth
Vanilla sugar natural 1 pinch / 0,5g. (yes)..*
Cinnamon ground 1 pinch / 0,5g. (recommended) ....*
Peppermint 2 leaves / 2g. (recommended) ....metal

Cooking instructions:
Add the cornstarch to a 1/2 cup apple juice.
Simmer the rhubarb in 1 cup of water for 10 min.
Add the remaining apple juice and the cornstarch, stir, heat till it boils again.
Sweet with honey and season with vanilla and cinnamon. Spread the mixture on dessert bowls and garnish with mint.

9.48 Rice dulse soup

Strengthens spleen and liver, regulates Qi flow, relaxes, builds up Qi, spreads, dries out, passes downwardly, strengthens stomach Qi, warms the stomach and spleen, harmonizes the intestine, forces Qi, reduces moisture.
Cooking time approx. 5 min
Calories p. portion: 190
2 portions
Allergens: L

Quantity of ingredients

Basic recipe for a rice soup (Congee) 4 cups / 500g. (reco.).............*
Basic recipe for a vegetable soup 2 cup / 500g. (recommended) ....*
Dulse (seaweed) 2 table spoons / 15g. (yes) ....water

Cooking instructions:
Worm up a portion of pre-cooked basic recipe for a ricesoupe (congee) and a portion pre-cooked basic recipe for a vegetable soup.
Bake the dulse in the oven at 220 degrees for 3 minutes. Spread the crisp dulse over the rice.

9.49 Rice porridge with orange peel

Warms the stomach and spleen, harmonizes the intestine, forces Qi, reduces moisture. brings the Liver Qi in motion, cools heat, moisturizes, relaxes, builds up Qi, spreads. nourishes blood, moisturizes, relaxes, builds up Qi, spreads.
Cooking time approx. 10 min
Calories p. portion: 120
4 portions
Allergens: L

Quantity of ingredients
Rice variety any 1 cup / 100g. (yes)...metal
Water 6 cups / 600g. (yes) .... earth
Orange grated peel 1/4 piece / 3g. (recommended)..........................*
Olive oil 1 table spoon / 10g. (recommended)........................... earth
Champignon 1/2 cup / 50g. (yes).. earth
Celery sticks 1/2 bunch / 60g. (recommended)......................... earth
Basic recipe for a chicken soup 3-4 table spoons / 40g. ....*
Salt 1 pinch / 0,5g. (little)...water

Cooking instructions:
The day before boil the rice with the orange peel and water in a ratio of about 1: 6. The amount of water determines the thickness of the mash (pure matter of taste). Put the rice in a saucepan with good insulation and a heavy lid. It is important to simmer the rice after a short boil on the slightest flame, otherwise it burns. Boil the rice for 2-4 hours. The longer he cooks, the more he strengthens.
Heat the oil in a saucepan, add the chopped champignon and celery and sauté briefly. Add the rice. Add vegetable broth or water, warm up, salt.

9.50 Rice with parsnips

Regulates Qi, dries out, passes downwardly, warms the stomach and spleen, harmonizes the intestine, forces Qi, reduces moisture. moisturizes, relaxes, builds up Qi, spreads. distributes mucus, activates Wei Qi, forces Qi.
Cooking time approx. 45 min
Calories p. portion: 206
3 portions

Quantity of ingredients
Rice variety any 1 cup / 120g. (yes)..metal
Water 1 1/2 cups / 200g. (yes)... earth
Salt 1 pinch / 1g. (little)...water
Parsnip 3-4 pieces / 450g. (recommended) .... fire
Olive oil 1 table spoon / 10g. (recommended)............................ earth
Sage 1 teaspoon / 3g. (recommended).. fire

Cooking instructions:
Peel the parsnips and cut into slices. Fry for a short time in oil. Add the
rice and fry again for a short time. Add the water and cook it at least 30
min. Sprinkle with fresh chopped sage.

9.51 Rice with stewed vegetables

Dissipates heat and moisture.
Cooking time approx. 20 min
Calories p. portion: 166
2 portions
Allergens: L

Quantity of ingredients
Rice variety any 1/2 cup / 60g. (yes)..metal
Water 3 cups / 300g. (yes) .... earth
Lemon peel 1 piece / 3g. (yes) .... fire
Water 1/2 cup / 0g. (yes).. earth
Carrot 2 pieces / 180g. (recommended).................................... earth
Celery sticks 1/2 piece / 5g. (recommended) .... earth
Champignon 1/2 cup / 50g. (yes).. earth
Cress 2 table spoons / 20g. (recommended) ....metal
Linseed oil 1 dash / 3g. (little)... earth

Cooking instructions:
Cook rice according to basic recipe with a piece of lemon peel.
Steam chopped carrots, celery and mushrooms until soft.
Then sprinkle with cress. Then add a dash of high quality cold oil.

9.52 Roasted millet with Celery sticks

Strengthens spleen and kidney, diuretic, brings the liver Qi in motion, cools heat, moisturizes, relaxes, builds up Qi, spreads.
Cooking time approx. 30 min
Calories p. portion: 400
2 portions
Allergens: L

Quantity of ingredients
Millet 1 cup / 120g. (yes) .... earth
Water 1 1/2 cups / 240g. (yes).. earth
Celery sticks 2 rods / 50g. (recommended).............................. earth
Water 2 table spoons / 30g. (yes)... earth
Herbs various 1 table spoon / 10g. (yes)... *
Salt 1 pinch / 1g. (little)..water
Sage 3-4 leaves / 2g. (recommended)... fire
Cress 1 teaspoon / 3g. (recommended)....................................metal

Cooking instructions:
Roast millet briefly, pour over water, heat till it boils and let stand for 20 min. to swell.

Cut celery into small pieces and mix with water, salt and fresh herbs and cook for 10 min. Add to the millet. Sprinkle fresh sage or watercress over it.

9.53 Roasted oatmeal with grapes compot

Moisturizes, relaxes, builds up Qi, spreads, forces Qi, warms the stomach and spleen, promotes blood circulation and conduction flow.
Cooking time approx. 25 min
Calories p. portion: 328
2 portions
Allergens: AO

Quantity of ingredients
Oat flakes roasted 1 cup / 120g. (yes) ....metal
Grapes red 1 1/2 cups / 240g. (recommended).......................... earth
Ginger fresh 1/2 teaspoon / 1g. (recommended).......................metal
Raisins 2 table spoons / 20g. (recommended)........................... earth
Cinnamon ground 1 pinch / 1g. (recommended) ....*
Water 1 1/2 cups / 200g. (yes)... earth

Cooking instructions:
Roast the oats briefly, pour over water, add raisins and cook while stirring for 20 min. Add grapes, ginger and cinnamon.

9.54 Rosemary Potatoes

Forces Qi, forces spleen, relieves inflammation, relaxes, builds up Qi, spreads.
Cooking time approx. 30 min
Calories p. portion: 188
2 portions

Quantity of ingredients
Potato 6-8 pieces / 420g. (recommended) .... earth
Salt (herbal) 1 pinch / 1g. (little) .... water
Olive oil 1 table spoon / 10g. (recommended) .... earth
Rosemary 1 teaspoon / 2g. (yes) .... fire

Cooking instructions:
Cut the potatoes into half´s, apply a little olive oil on the cut surface, then salt, sprinkle 2 - 3 rosemary needles on the potatoes.
Place the potatoes on the baking tray and bake them in the preheated oven for approx. 25 minutes to 190°C/374°F.

9.55 Spring salad

Preserves the fluids, nourishes liver-Yin, cools heat, produces humors, moves Qi and blood, diuretic, cools in internal heat, dissolves stagnation, passes downwardly.
Cooking time approx. 10 min
Calories p. portion: 162
4 portions
Allergens: AEMN

Quantity of ingredients
Sorrel 3/8 lbs - 6oz / 150g. (yes) .... wood
Dandelion (young plants) 1/4 lbs - 4oz / 100g. (recommended) ..... fire
Mung bean sprouting 0,2 lbs / 75g. (recommended) .... water
Cress 1/4 lbs - 4oz / 100g. (recommended) .... metal
Chives 1 Bunch / 50g. (recommended) .... metal

Tomato 2 pieces / 100g. (recommended) .... wood
Parsley 1 Bunch / 50g. (recommended).................................... wood
Sesame paste (Tahini) 2 table spoons / 16g. (little)................... earth
Soy sauce 1 dash / 3g. (yes) .... water
Mustard 1/2 teaspoon / 2g. (yes) .... metal
White bread (wheat bread) 6 slices / 120g. (yes) .... wood

Cooking instructions:
Wash all salad´s, mix and prepare the sauce as follows:
Mix tahini with mustard and balsamic vinegar, tamari, olive oil, chives
and half of parsley. Pour the sauce over the salad and sprinkle the
remaining parsley just before serving.
Serve with the white bread.

9.56 Strawberry soup with melons

Forces blood, cools blood, preserves the fluids, contracts, moisturizes,
spreads, forces heart Yin.
Cooking time approx. 5 min
Calories p. portion: 87
2 portions

Quantity of ingredients
Strawberries 3/4 lbs / 300g. (recommended) .... wood
Strawberry Juice 1/3 cup / 70g. (recommended)........................ wood
Lemon peel 1/4 teaspoon / 1g. (yes).. fire
Cantaloupe 5/8 oz / 200g. (yes).. earth

Cooking instructions:
Puree strawberries (fresh or frozen) and strawberry juice with the
blender, mix in a little sugar.
Cut melon pulp into small pieces.
Arrange strawberry soup in portions. Put the melon cubes in the sweet
soup.

9.57 Tea from anise

Warms the middle, forces stomach and spleen, warms stomach,
reduces cold-evil, harmonizes stomach-Qi, warms kidney.
Cooking time approx. 15 min
Calories p. portion: 3
4 portions

Quantity of ingredients
Anise (Common Fennel) 1 teaspoon / 3g. (recommended) .... earth
Water 2 cup / 500g. (yes) .... earth

Cooking instructions:
Heat the water till it boils and put it aside. Add anise.
10 min. to let go.
Pour through a tea strainer. Sweet to taste with honey.

In order to achieve a salutary effect, you should drink 2 cups of anise
tea per day.

9.58 Tea from ginseng

Forces heart, lungs, stomach, spleen, kidney-Qi.
Cooking time approx. 20 min
Calories p. portion: 0
4 portions

Quantity of ingredients
Ginseng 2 teabags / 4g. (recommended) ....*
Water 2 cup / 500g. (yes) .... earth

Cooking instructions:
A very mild form of taking ginseng is achieved by placing it in a thermos
of hot water. You can also use the root several times, not just for a pot
filling. Ideally, you should have cooked the water for 10 minutes - it is
then assigned to the conversion phase of fire - and to use non-
carbonated medicinal spring water, if the quality of the water on site is
not good.

Ingestion: This mild ginseng tea can be drunk throughout the day for
strengthening.

9.59 Tea from rose hip

Strengthens spleen Qi.
Cooking time approx. 10 min
Calories p. portion: 2
4 portions

Quantity of ingredients
Rose hip tea 2 table spoons / 4g. (recommended) .... wood
Water 2 cup / 500g. (yes) .... earth

Cooking instructions:
Heat the water till it boils and put it aside. Add rosehip and leave for 10 min. to let go. Sweet to taste with honey. Strain when pouring.

9.60 Tea from sage

Distributes mucus, passes downwardly, activates Wei Qi, forces Qi.
Cooking time approx. 15 min
Calories p. portion: 4
4 portions

Quantity of ingredients
Sage 2 teaspoons / 6g. (recommended)...................................... fire
Water 2 cup / 500g. (yes)... earth

Cooking instructions:
Heat the water till it boils and put it aside. Add sage and 10 min. to let go. Strain. Sweet to taste with honey.

9.61 Tea Green tea

Reduces internal heat, dissolves mucus, detoxifies.
Cooking time approx. 10 min
Calories p. portion: 2
1 portions

Quantity of ingredients
Green tea 1 teaspoon / 2g. (recommended) .... fire
Water 1 cup / 120g. (yes)... earth

Cooking instructions:
For each cup you use a teaspoonful or a teabag.
Pour green tea only with 60 to 80 ° C / 140 to 176 °F hot water, otherwise it will be bitter.
If the tea has a stimulating effect, let it draw for two to three minutes. It has a calming effect for a duration of five minutes (no longer, otherwise it will be bitter!).
Another method: Pour the tea leaves with about 70 ° C / 158 °F hot water and pour the water immediately again. Then just pour hot water again. The bitter substances disappear and the tea gets a milder aroma.

9.62 Vegetable juice

Nourishes liver-Yin, cools heat, produces humors, strengthens spleen and liver, regulates Qi flow, moisturizes, relaxes, strengthens stomach Qi, relaxes, builds up Qi, spreads.
Cooking time approx. 15 min
Calories p. portion: 64
1 portions
Allergens: L

Quantity of ingredients
Celery root 1/2 oz / 20g. (recommended).................................. earth
Carrot 1/4 lbs - 4oz / 100g. (recommended)............................. earth
Tomato 1/4 lbs - 4oz / 100g. (recommended) ....wood
Garlic 1 piece / 2g. (recommended)...metal
Salt 1 teaspoon / 2g. (little)...water
Acerola fruit nectar or powder 1/2 teaspoon / 1g. (yes).............. wood

Cooking instructions:
Peel all ingredients and use the juicer to make a drink. Stir in the acerola.

9.63 Whole milk cereal mash

Nourishes fluids, moisturises dryness, produces humors, moisturizes intestines, cools inner heat, forces the middle, nourishes liver-blood, preserves the fluids, contracts.
Cooking time approx. 20 min
Calories p. portion: 205
1 portions
Allergens: AG

Quantity of ingredients
Cow's milk (whole milk 3.5% fat) 3/4 cup - 6 oz / 200g. (yes) ....*
Water 1/4 cup / 50g. (yes) .... earth
Spelled flakes 1/2 oz / 20g. (recommended).............................wood
Fruit mix juice 1/2 oz / 20g. (recommended) ....*

Cooking instructions:
Boil the milk with the wholegrain flakes and let it swell. Add the pureed fruit.
Switch between wheat, oats and wholemeal spelled flakes, as well as the fruits. So you get a variety of flavors.

10 Effects of food

10.1 Use ingredients: recommendable

Acai powder
Adzuki beans
Agar agar (kelp)
Aloe juice
Angelica root
Anise (Common Fennel)
Apple (sour)
Apple (sweet)
Apple puree
Arrowroot
Artichoke
Asparagus (green or white)
Aubergine
Banchatee (green tea)
barberry
Basic recipe for a beef soup
Basic recipe for a beef soup (warming)
Basic recipe for a chicken soup (warming)
Basic recipe for a fish soup
Basic recipe for a rice soup (Congee)
Basic recipe for a vegetable soup (nutritious)
Basil
Basil (fresh)
Batavia
Bay leaf
Beans (green, fresh)
Bearberry leaf
Beef meatbones
Beer (alcohol-free)
Beer (alcohol-reduced)
Berries of the season
Berry juice
Bitter Herb liqueur
Bitter liqueur
Black beans
Blackberry dried (unripe fruit)
Blackberry´s
Black-eyed peas
Blueberry
Blueberry juice
Borage
Boxhorn clover seeds
Bread with carob kernel flour
Buckwheat
Buckwheat (roasted) Kasha
Bulgur (cereals)
Burdock root tea

Cardamom
Carrot
Carrot (Early Carrot)
Carrot juice without sugar
Celery root
Celery sticks
Chamomile tea
Channa-Dal
Chard
Chenpi (chinese tangerine bowl)
Chervil
Chervil dried
Chicken Blood
Chicken stomach
Chickweed
Chicory
Chinese cabbage
Chinese pearl barley
Chives
Chlorella (fresh water)
Chrysanthemum blossom tea
Cinnamon ground
Cinnamon sticks
Clove
Cod
Codfish
Coix (seeds) YiYi Ren
Compote (fruits of the season)
Coriander
Corn (roasted)
Corn silk tea
Cottage cheese
Crab
Cranberry
Cranberry juice
Cream 10% coffee cream
Cream sour 10%
Cress
Crucian
Cucumber (bitter)
Cumin (Caraway seed)
Curcuma
Currant (black)
Currant (red)
Currant (white)
Currant juice (black)
Daisy
Dandelion (young plants)
Dandelionroots tea

Deer meat
Deer meat
Deer's Bones
Deer's kidneys
Dill
Dyer's broom herb
Elderberries
Elderberry blossom tee
Endive salad
Fennel
Fernet Branca (herbal bitter liqueur)
Fish innards
Fish remains
Flower pollen
Fox nut, gorgon nut, makhana
Freshwater crab
Freshwater fish
Fructose (glucose)
Fruit mix juice
Gail plum
Galangal
Garam Masala powder
Garlic
Gelatin white
Gelee Royal
Gentian root tea
Ginger fresh
Ginseng
Ginseng liqueur
Goat
Goat and sheep's blood
Goat and sheep's brain
Goat and sheep's liver
Goat and sheep's milk
Goat and sheep's stomach
Goose blood
Gooseberry
Gourd
Grape juice red
Grapefruit dried peel
Grapes red
Grapes white
Grass carp
Green spelt
Green tea
Ground caraway
Guava
Hawthorn
Herbal tea mix
Herbs bitter
Herbs of Provence
Herbs wild
Hibiscus
Hibiscus tea

Hokkaido pumpkin
Honey
Horse meat
Hyssop
Jasmine blossoms tee
Jellyfish
Juniper berry
King Solomon's-seal
Kombu seaweed (Saccharina japonica)
Kudzu
Kukicha tea
Kumquats
Lamb bones
Lamb kidneys
Lamb's lettuce
Lamb's lettuce
Licorice root tea
Lily bulbs
Liver smoothing tea
Loquate / Japanese medlar
Lotus roots
Lotus seeds
Lovage
Lovage seeds
Luo Han Guo fruit
Lychee
Lychee in Preserved
Lychee liqueur
Mackerel
Mallow (Malva sylvestris) blossom tea
Maple syrup
Mare's milk
Mascarpone cheese
Mediterranean fish (cod, plaice, haddock, sea eel, mackerel)
Mineral water
Miso black (fermented)
Morel, dried
Mu Erh Mushroom
Mung bean sprouting
Mustard seeds
Nasturtium (nose-twister or nose-tweaker)
Nettles
Nori, purple seaweed, red algae
Octopus
Olive oil
Orange blossom
Orange dried peel
Orange grated peel
Oregano dried
Oregano fresh
Oyster shell powder
Parsley

Parsnip
Passion blossoms tea
Pearl barley
Peas
Peas, green
Pepper powder (hot)
Peppermint
Peppermint tea
Peppers (sweet)
Perch
Pheasant
Pig blood
Pigeon
Pigeon egg
Pinto beans speckled
Plaice
Pork Bacon
Pork brain
Pork lung
Pork marrow bones
Pork skin
Pork stomach
Pork's intestine
Potato
Potato (mealy)
Potato flour
Prickly pear
Processed cheese 12%
Pumpkin
Quail
Quince
Rabbit
Rabbit (wild)
Rabbit liver
Rabbit meat
Radicchio
Radish
Radish (white, green, purple-red)
Radish horseradish
Radish leaves
Raisins
Raspberry
Raspberry dried (immature)
Raspberry leaf tea
Red beet
Rhubarb
Rice (Gaoliang / Sorghum)
Rice black
Rice noodles
Rice red
Rice sweet
Romaine lettuce / lettuce salad
Rose blossom tea
Rose hip

Rose hip tea
Rose leaf tea
Rosefish
Rucola
Safflower (Dyer's thistle / Hong Hua)
Sage
Salsify
Savory
Sea cucumber
Seacrab
Shark
Sheep's milk yoghurt
Slug
Sour milk
Soy noodles
Spelled (Dark) bread
Spelled flakes
Spelled semolina
Spelled wholemeal flour
Spiny lobsters
Spirit
St. Benedict's thistle, blessed thistle,
holy thistle, spotted thistle
Star anise
Strawberries
Strawberry Juice
Sugar substitute (sweetener)
Tea mixture uric acid lowering
Thyme
Thyme dried
Tomato
Tomato juice
Tomato paste
Tomato puree
Trout
Turmeric (yellow root)
Turnip
Turnips
Vanilla
Vanilla powder
Vegetable juice
Vinegar (Apple vinegar)
Vinegar Aceto Balsamico
Wakame
Watermelon
Wax gourd
Wheatgrass juice
Wheatgrass powder
Whey
Whitefish
Wholemeal flour
Wild boar meat
Wild garlic (garlic spinach)
Wild herbs

Wild strawberries
Yam root, yam root tuber
Yew nut
Yoghurt vanilla

Yogurt (natural, 1.5% fat)
Yogurt (natural, 3.5% fat)
Zucchini

10.2 Use ingredients: yes

Acerola fruit nectar or powder
Agave nectar
Agrimony
Amaranth
Amaranth Pops
Anchovy / Sardine
Apple juice (natural cloudy)
Apricot
Baking powder
Balm
Bamboo shoots
Banana
Banana (cooking banana)
Barley
Barley flour
Barley grass powder
Barley grouts
Barley malt
Barley not peeled
Basic recipe for a duck soup
Beef fillet
Beef heart
Beef heart (calf)
Beef lungs (calf)
Beef meat
Beef meat (calf)
Beef Oxtail pieces
Beef soup meat
Beef stomach
Bitter Lemon
Bitter orange peel
Black caraway
Black tea
Blackberry jam
Blackberry leaves
Blackthorn (Sloe)
Blue mallow tee
Blueberry dried
Blueberry jam
Bocksdorn fruits (Fructus Lycii, Goji, goji berry dried
Bread roll
Breadcrumbs (wheat bread, bread roll)
Buckbean
Buckwheat whole grain
Buttermilk
Calamari

Cantaloupe
Capers in olive oil
Carambola (Star fruit)
Carp
Caviar
Cereal coffee
Chamomile
Champignon
Chestnut puree
Chestnuts
Chicken egg
Chicken egg white
Chicken heart
Chicken meat
Chili (pod or ground)
Chocolate (Diabetic)
Clementine
Clementines
Cocoa
Coconut milk
Cola drink
Cola drink (low calorie)
Coriander (fresh)
Corn
Corn (fast polenta)
Corn flour
Corn Grease (Polenta)
Corn starch
Couscous
Cow's milk (1.5% fat)
Cow's milk (whole milk 3.5% fat)
Cranberries
Cranberry
Cranberry jam
Creamer
Crispbread
Currant jam (black)
Currant jam (red)
Currants (black)
Currants (red)
Curry
Curry paste red
Dandelion juice
Dashi
Duck (heart)
Ducks egg
Dulse (seaweed)

Fennel seeds ground
Fennel tea
Fenugreek (Trigonella foenum-
graecum)
Fig
Fig dried
Fish pieces mixed (fresh water)
Fish sauce
Flounder
Fruit tea
Gentian root
Ginger powder
Ginkgo fruit
Ginseng root
Goose egg
Grape juice white
Grapefruit (Pomelo)
Grapefruit juice
Ground
Halibut (Flatfish)
Herbs various
Hijiki
Hop
Horehound leaves
Iceberg lettuce
Kaki plum
Kalmus
Kefir
Kiwi
Ladyfingers
Lavender blossoms
Leaf salads (bitter)
Lemon
Lemon Balm (dried)
Lemon Balm (fresh)
Lemon juice
Lemon peel
Lemongrass
Lettuce
Lime
Lime blossom tea
Lobster
Longane
Lye roll
Malt
Mango juice
Manioc flour
Marjoram
Medlar
Millet
Millet flakes
Miso
Miso paste (soy bean paste)
Mixed Pickles

Mozzarella
Mulberry fruit
Mulled Wine Spice
Mullet
Mussels
Mustard
Mustard Dijon
Mustard medium hot
Mustard sweet
Mutton
Nectarine
Noodles (wheat) with egg
Noodles (wheat, lasagne) with egg
Noodles (wheat, ribbon noodles) with
egg
Noodles (wheat, spaghetti) with egg
Oat
Oat flakes roasted
Oat flour
Oat meal
Oat milk
Octopus
Orange
Orange jam
Orange juice
Orange peel
Oysters
Papaya
Parmesan
Parsley root
Passion fruit
Pearl barley
Pepper (ground)
Pepper Cayenne
Pepper white (ground)
Peppercorns
Peppers powder
Pickle
Pimento
Pineapple
Pineapple juice without sugar
Pomegranate
Pork ham
Pork ham cooked
Pork ham smoked
Pork sausage (Bratwurst) Pork/beef
sausage (smoked)
Psyllium seed
Pudding powder vanilla
Puff pastry
Pumpernickel (dark bread)
Quail egg
Quinoa
Radish black

Raspberry jam
Red berry (without sugar)
Red wine
Reishi mushroom
Ribworttea
Rice (fragrance)
Rice (whole grain)
Rice Basmati
Rice flour
Rice long grain rice
Rice malt
Rice round grain
Rice starch
Rice sticky
Rice variety any
Rosemary
Rusk
Rye
Rye flour
Rye wholemeal bread
Saffron
Sago (cereals)
Salmon
Sea buckthorn
Sesame, black
Sheep's milk
Shrimp
Shrimps
Skim milk powder
Sorrel
Sourdough
Soy sauce
Spelled grain
Spinach
Spurdog (spiny dogfish, Schillerlocken)
Stevia (candyleaf, sweetleaf)
Strawberry jam
Sugar brown
Sugar cane sugar
Sugar fructose - fruit sugar
Sugar glucose - grapes sugar
Sugar Milk Sugar
Sugar molasses
Supplementary nutrition
Sweet potato

Tabasco
Tangerine
Tarragon (Estragon)
Toast bread (whole grain)
Tomato dried
Tonic Water
Topinambur
Trout (smoked)
Truffle
Tsampa (roasted barley flour)
Turkey breast meat
Turkey ham
Umeboshi paste
Umeboshi plums (Japanese apricots)
Valerian
Vanilla pod
Vanilla sugar natural
Vinegar (Red wine vinegar)
Vinegar Aceto Balsamico white
Water
Water hot
Wheat
Wheat bran
Wheat bulgur
Wheat flakes
Wheat flatbread/pita bread
Wheat flour
Wheat flour whole grain
Wheat semolina
Wheat semolina for children
Wheat/Rye/Gray-black bread with yeast
White bread (baguette)
White bread (pretzel sticks)
White bread (roll)
White bread (wheat bread)
White breadcrumbs
White dumpling bread (wheat bread cut into chunks)
Wormwood
Wormwood herb
Yarrow
Yarrow tea
Yeast
Yogi tea

10.3 Use ingredients: little

Avocado
Bean oil
Beef kidney
Beef liver
Borage oil

Brie cheese
Broccoli
Brown ale
Brussels sprouts
Camembert

Carob flour, St. john's bread
Cauliflower
Chicken liver
Chicken yolk
Chickpeas
Clarified butter
Coconut fat
Coconut flakes
Coconut grated
Coconut meat
Cooking oil
Corn germ oil
Cream sour 20%
Cream, sweet 30%
Cucumber
Cucumber (spicy cucumber)
Curd cheese 20%
Duck (slaughtered)
Edam cheese
Emmental cheese
Evening primrose oil
Feta cheese
Feta cheese
Fresh cheese
Fresh cheese from soya
Fresh cheese with herbs
Ginger oil
Gouda cheese
Grapeseed oil
Hazelnuts
Herring
Honey wine (Met)
Kohlrabi
Lamb liver
Lamb meat
Lamb shoulder
Lentils
Lentils red
Lentils yellow
Linseed
Linseed (crushed)
Linseed oil
Muesli
Multi-grain bread (gray bread)
Mutton
Noodles (whole grain) with egg
Nutmeg
Olives
Olives green
Onion (spring onion)
Palm oil
Peanut (roasted)
Peanut oil

Peanuts
Pepperoni
Pepperoni, red, pitted, halved
Pepperoni, yellow, pitted, halved
Peppers (rose peppers)
Pineapple (from a can)
Poppy
Pork heart
Pork kidneys
Pork knuckle
Pork liver
Pork meat
processed cheese 30%
Prosecco
Pumpkin seed oil
Pumpkin seeds
Rapeseed oil
Rice mash
Rice wild (nature rice)
Sake
Salt
Salt (herbal)
Sesame oil
Sesame oil roasted
Sesame paste (Tahini)
Sesame, white
Sour cream 15% fat
Sour milk cheese 20%
Soy flour
Soy Tofu
Soy Tofu smoked
Soya Cuisine (soy cream)
Soybean milk
Soybean oil
Soybeans
Soybeans, black
Soybeans, blacks, fermented
Soybeans, yellow
Sugar - icing sugar
Sugar candy white
Sugar palm sugar
Sugar white
Sunflower seeds
Thistle oil
Tuna
Walnut oil
Wheat beer
Wheat germ oil

10.4 Do not use contra-acting foods

Almond
Almond marzipan
Almond milk
Almond puree
Apricot dried
Apricot jam
Apricot nectar
Apricots
Apricots juice
Beef bone marrow
Beer (Pils)
Beer (Top-fermented German dark beer)
Black fungus mushroom
Boletus mushroom
Brazil nuts
Broad beans (thick beans)
Bush beans
Butter (half fat)
Butter beans white
Butter organic
Campari
Cashews
Chanterelle
Cherry
Cherry (sour)
Cherry compote
Cherry juice
Chocolate
Coffee
Cream (30% fat)
Cream sour 30%
Créme fraiche cheese
Curd cheese 40%
Dates dried
Dates red
Eel
Eel smoked
French beans
Goat cheese
Goose
Goose fat
Goose parts
Gorgonzola
Greengage
Kidney beans (red)
Leek

Lentils black
Lima beans
Mango
Margarine
Margarine (diet)
Martini
Mayonnaise 50%
Mayonnaise 80%
Mirabelle plum
Mold cheese
Morel (black, dried)
Mung bean
Oat flakes (whole grain)
Oat fusion (baby food)
Okra
Onion (shallot)
Onion read
Onion white
Oyster mushroom
Peaches
Peaches (canned)
Peanut butter
Pear
Pear juice
Peppers
Pine nuts
Pistachios
Plum
Plum dried
Plums
Pork fat (lard)
Pork Lard
Red cabbage
Rum
Sauerkraut (cutted cabbage fermented)
Savoy cabbage / kale
Sherry (whine)
Shiitake, dried
Sour cherries
Sunflower oil
Walnuts
Walnuts roasted
White beans
White cabbage
White wine
Whole grain bread

11 Herbs and their effects

11.1 Basil

thermal effect: warm
taste: spicy, bitter
Dries out, leads down. Tonifies Yang and Qi, dissolves mucus-cold, eliminates wind-cold.
It has a beneficial effect on flatulence and nausea, relaxing and soothing. Good to fight emphysema, bronchitis, whooping cough, high blood pressure, headache, mouth odor, warts, hiccup, gout, migraine.

11.2 Mugwort

thermal effect: warm
taste: bitter, spicy
Regulates and nourishes bleeding, warms the inside, eliminates wind-cold, eliminates parasites, eliminates heat, wetness, regulates and moves Qi.
Reduces bleeding, alleviates pain. In the kitchen, mugwort is used as a spice for fat food. Since it contains many bitter substances, it boosts fat burning and promotes digestion.

11.3 Savory

thermal effect: warm
taste: bitter
Tonifies kidney yang, heart qi, stomach and spleen qi and warms the middle, moves the liver qi and blood, releases mucous and cold from the lungs, opens the surface, induces wind-cold.
Stomach-strengthening, soothing and appetizing. Ideal for prevent colds, strengthens the immune system. In case of incontinence or nocturnal wetting (not for children), put the beans in liquor for libido.

11.4 Nettles

thermal effect: neutral
taste: bitter
Lowers Qi, dries out, direct down. Tonifies Yang, dissolves / transforms mucus, regulates and moves qi, eliminates wind-cold / heat-wetness.
Promotes urination. Tea or juice, cleanses the blood and the kidneys, supports prostate problems, inhibit the formation of inflammation, pain-relieving.

11.5 Coriander

thermal effect: warm
taste: spicy
Driving sweat, reducing wind, draining moisture, tonifying and regulating qi, eliminating wind-cold.
The essential oils are appetizing, digestive, cramping and soothing in stomach and intestinal disorders.

11.6 Herbs various

Stimulates appetite. Effect different.
Appetizing, lots of trace elements and vitamins.

11.7 Cress

thermal effect: cool
taste: sweet
Moves and tonifies qi and blood, diuretic, cools in internal heat, moisturizes lungs, triggers stagnation, heads upwards.
Diuretic, supports urination. Good to fight dry mouth, inner agitation, sore throat, diabetes, kidney stones, gastrointestinal complaints, lung problems, menstrual cramps or cancer.

11.8 Chives

thermal effect: warm
taste: spicy
Directs upward. Tonifies blood, kidney Yang and Qi. Dissolves moisture. Bactericide, prevents cancer, strengthens gastric juice production, promotes digestion and blood circulation, promotes growth, triggers stagnation.

11.9 Lovage

thermal effect: warm
taste: spicy, bitter
Reduces inner wind and moisture, dissolves stagnation, directs upward, warms Yang, regulates and moves Qi, warms inside, dissolves mucus-cold, eliminates wind-cold.
Stimulates digestion, reduces pain. Extracts of the root are used to flush out urinary tract infections and prevent kidney gravel.

11.10   Lily bulbs

thermal effect: cool
taste: sweet, bitter
Tonifies Yin, soothes Shen / Spirit. Moisturizes the lungs, clears heat and
stops coughing.
Calms nerves, good to fight scaly skin. The onions and the petals are
added to ointments in the Orient, which can heal muscles and tendons.
White lily (astringent).

11.11   Dandelion (young plants)

thermal effect: cool
taste: sweet, bitter
Cools liver-heat, reduces internal heat, softens knots, eliminates heat,
reduces fire, dissolves mucus heat, moves blood, tonifies qi.
Detoxifies, relieves inflammation. Regulates digestion, helps with
rheumatism, releases kidney stones, leaves pimples and chronic skin
disorders disappear.

11.12   Parsley

thermal effect: warm
taste: bitter
Nourishes blood and liver, harmonizes liver and spleen, strengthens
eyesight, preserves juices, contracts. Dissolves moisture and warms
Yang.
Stimulates liver function, detoxifies. Forces urinating. Relieves flatulence.
Digestive and menstrual stimulating, birth-
accelerating, memory-enhancing, blood-purifying, skin-smoothing.

11.13   Peppermint

thermal effect: cool
taste: spicy, bitter
Cools heat, expels mucus, dissipates wind-cold and wind-heat, moves
stomach qi, releases congestion, tonifies, regulates and moves qi.
Relaxes, frees the lungs and the nose (inhale), regulates the cycle.
Stimulates bile flow and bile production, antispasmodic in gastrointestinal
disorders, antimicrobial and antiviral.

11.14   Rosemary

thermal effect: warm
taste: bitter
Dries out, leads down. Strengthens the heart, lungs and spleen qi,
strengthens liver blood. Strengthens heart-Yin. Expels spleen heat / cold
moisture. Strengthens spleen and kidney yang.
Promotes digestion, relieves bloating, strengthens lung, spleen and
kidney. Affects the circulation and nerves. Appetizing. Baths help to fight
circulatory disorders as well as with gout and rheumatism.

11.15   Sage

thermal effect: neutral
taste: bitter, spicy
Expels slime, guides down, strengthens Qi, eliminates Wind-Heat,
eliminate heat induced by Yin deficiency.
Good to fight yeast infections. The leaves have a digestive effect and are
used in greasy foods. Antiperspirant effect. Helps to relieve coughing
attacks. Dries out.

11.16   Sorrel

thermal effect: cold
taste: sour
Protects the fluids, pull together.
Astringent, hematopoietic, purifies the blood, diuretic. Good to fight liver
weakness, upset stomach, indigestion, constipation, diarrhea, worms,
scurvy, anemia, women's complaints, wounds, skin rashes, boils, ulcers,
swelling.

11.17   Thyme dried

thermal effect: warm
taste: bitter
Strengthens the lungs and spleen. Clears wind-cold, dissolves slime-cold,
tones qi, soothes Shen / Spirit.
Disinfecting. It stimulates the blood circulation, increases the appetite and
helps to digest fat meat better. Strengthens lungs and spleen.

11.18   King Solomon's-seal

thermal effect: neutral
taste: sweet, bitter
Tonifies Yin and Qi, astringent, tonifies blood, eliminates wind-cold / heat-wetness.
Used to repair wounds or damaged tissue. Good to fight dry cough, earlier also tuberculosis and dysentery, as well as diarrhea and hemorrhoids.

11.19   Yam root, yam root tuber

thermal effect: neutral
taste: sweet
Tonifies Yin, Yang and Qi, reduces inner wind, dissolves wetness, warms Yang.
Solves cramps (in the gastrointestinal tract). Digestive through increased bile production. Anti-inflammatory in rheumatic diseases.
Mucolytic agent for coughing. Relief of menopausal symptoms.

12 Basics of Nutrition

The basic principles of nutrition described herein are general recommendations. They are not aimed at a specific form of therapy. Recommendations concerning a therapy have priority.

12.1 Nutrition

Regular meals in a relaxed atmosphere. A warm breakfast is considered a good start into the day.
The main meals ought to be taken for lunch – supper in the early evening. Pay attention to feeling hungry or sated: don't eat too much nor remain hungry is the rule
Prepare the meals freshly from natural, regional products. Frozen, heat-conserved, industrially prepared or foodstuffs cooked in the microwave oven are rejected.
Choice of foodstuffs according to the season: more cooling food in summer, more warming food in winter.
Eat cooked food at least twice a day. Food and drinks ought to be lukewarm, never ice-cold or hot.
Raw vegetables, briefly cooked vegetables, freshly squeezed juices and mineral water are not recommended. Milk and dairy products are only included in the diet if they don't cause problems. Don't use therapeutic recipes over a longer period without consulting your doctor or therapist.

Varied food
Enjoy the diversity of foodstuffs. Characteristics of a balanced nutrition are variety, suitable combination and a balanced quantity of rich and low energy foodstuffs (on one hand avoiding undersupply with essential nutrients and on the other hand to take to many undesirable substances).

A lot of Cereal Products - and Potatoes
Bread, pasta, rice, cereal flakes (best wholemeal) as well as potatoes contain almost no fat, but many vitamins, mineral nutrients, trace elements, roughage and secondary plant substances. These foodstuffs ought to be taken with low-fat side dishes.

Vegetables and Fruit – „Take Five" every day ... 5 portions of
vegetables and fruit a day, as fresh as possible, briefly cooked, or maybe one portion as a juice – ideal as a side dish to every meal as well as snack between meals: Thus a lot of vitamins, mineral nutrients as well as roughage and secondary plant substances

Daily milk and dairy products

Milk and Dairy Products every Day, once or twice per Week Fish; meat, sausages as well as eggs moderately. These foodstuffs contain valuable nutrients like calcium in the milk, iodine selenium and omega-3 fat acids in saltwater fish. Meat is favorable due to its high content of disposable iron and the vitamins B1, B6 and B12. Quantities of 300 – 600 g meat and sausage per week are sufficient. Prefer low-fat products, especially in meat- and dairy products.

Low-fat and fatty Foodstuffs

Fat supplies us with essential fat acids and fatty foodstuffs contain also fat-soluble vitamins. Fat is high in energy; therefore much fat in the food may cause overweight, possibly also cancer. Too many saturated fat acids may further a tendency for cardio-vascular diseases in the long term. Prefer vegetable oils and fats (e.g. rapeseed-, olive-, soya-oils and solid fats produced therefrom). Beware of invisible fat in meat- and dairy products, pastry and sweets as well as in fast-food and convenience foods. 70 – 90 g fat per day is sufficient.

Moderately Sugar and Salt

Take sugar and foods/drinks containing various kinds of sugar (e.g. glucose syrup) only occasionally. Use herbs and spices as well as a little salt creatively. Prefer salt containing iodine.

Plenty of Liquids

Water is absolutely essential. Drink 1-2 l liquids every day. Prefer water (with or without gas) and other low-calorie drinks. Alcoholic drinks should not be taken.

Tasty Dishes, carefully cooked

Cook the meals with as low temperatures and as short as possible, using little water and fat – this preserves the original taste, keeps the nutrients intact and prevents the production of harmful compounds.

Take time and enjoy the food

Take your Time and enjoy your Food
Eating consciously helps to eat right. The eye enjoys food, too. It's fun, invites to enjoy varied dishes and stimulates the feeling of satiety.

Watch your Weight and stay in Motion

A balanced diet and a lot of exercise and sport (30 – 60 min/day) are a healthy combination. The right weight furthers well-being and health. Thermals, directional effectiveness, digestive power

There are various criteria for judging the effectiveness of herbs and foodstuffs.

The use of certain herbs and ingredients is based on observations of the effects on the body which these foodstuffs, herbs and spices show after having eaten them. The medical science has developed following system: Every ingredient or herb has a directional effectiveness. Furthermore, there are herbs which have a special effect on certain organs.

The basic condition for a healthy metabolism is to obtain sufficient energy from food and that the digestive process doesn't use too much energy. An easily digestible meal makes content and sated, doesn't cause flatulence and fatigue after the meal. The perfect spices increase the healthiness of our meals. Very often, just small doses of herbs and spices will suffice. They are not used to make us sated, but to help our digestive organs to digest the food.

12.2 Recipes

The recipes list the ingredients to be used and the cooking instructions show how the dish is prepared. The list of ingredients shows the concerned quantities as well as the relevance for the therapy. If you find „less than mentioned", try to comply or find an alternative from the „list of recommended foodstuffs". Mostly it shall result just in a small change of taste when you simply avoid this ingredient.

Mild cooking methods: boiling, stewing, poaching, steaming
Strong cooking methods: barbecuing, roasting, frying, smoking
Balanced cooking methods: deep-frying, baking brick
Deep-freezing and warming in the microwave oven should be avoided (denaturalization).

12.3 Foodstuffs

Foodstuffs have an effect on body and soul like medicinal herbs, only a very much milder one. Dietary advice is mainly based on regional foodstuffs. The knowledge about the effects of each foodstuff and the knowledge, when which foodstuff shall be used, is based on the orthodox school of medicine. Use ecologic-organic products, if possible. As everything should be cooked for a long time due to a better digestability and very rarely eaten raw, the food agrees with everyone.

The classification of the foodstuffs according to their effect on the body is the basis in order to achieve a harmonious status of health.

Dietary advisors do not recommend certain foodstuffs for everyone. The individual diet is tailor-made for the individual constitution.

Buy only fresh and ripe fruit and vegetables. You ought to leave unripe fruit and vegetables and such with brown spots and wilted leaves behind in the market. In this case take deep-frozen goods (never ready-to-serve dishes!). Fruit and vegetables are deep-frozen immediately after harvesting and often contain more vitamins and minerals than the goods from the vegetable shelf. Whereas conserved or tinned goods contain very much less biological substances. Also, salt, sugar and others are mostly added to the latter. Never leave the foodstuffs in the water after washing them to avoid that many vital substances get drowned. Clean salads, fruit and vegetables immediately before serving.

Please make sure of the hygienic processing of foodstuffs. Clean your salads, fruit and vegetables carefully. When cooking with meat, prepare all ingredients first and then process the meat products. Clean the worktop and tools very carefully. Wooden surfaces ought to be treated with a mild disinfectant regularly in order to reduce germination.
Store fruit and vegetables separately, if possible. Harvested fruit and vegetables are still alive and emit e.g. ethylene gas, which makes other products ripen and age faster. Keep meat and fish in the closed packaging or store them in the fridge in closed containers.

12.4 Herbs

There are some basic rules for storing medicinal herbs. On principle, herbs must be protected from direct sunlight, humidity and heat.

Containers for the storage of herbs may be glasses, ceramic jars and even plastic containers. However, plastic is a rather unsuitable material and should only be a short-term solution. In case of glass containers, use a dark material.

Medicinal herbs cannot be kept for any long period. The shelf life of herbs is limited. However, it can be prolonged with suitable storage. The place should be dark, rather cool and absolutely dry. A wooden medicine cabinet, placed not directly next to a source of heat, would be ideal. Never buy large quantities of herbs so as not to have to throw them away. Label the container with the name of the herb and the date of harvesting or processing.

13 Other dietic-books

The following syndromes of dietetics, TCM or for a therapy supplement for cancer are available.

Dietetics
E001. Nutrition of the infant - baby food
E002. Nutrition during lactation
E003. Nutrition in old age
E004. Nutrition of children and adolescents
E005. Nutrition of athletes
E006. Light weight
E007. Pregnancy
E008. Full food

Protein and electrolyte - kidneys
E009. (hemodialysis) dialysis treatment
E010. Acute renal failure
E011. Chronic renal insufficiency
E012. Nephrotic syndrome
E013. Kidney stones (nephrolithiasis)

Gastrointestinal tract - pancreas
E014. Acute pancreatitis (inflammation of the pancreas)
E015. Chronic pancreatitis (inflammation of the pancreas)

Gastrointestinal tract - small intestine and large intestine
E016. Acute obstipation (constipation)
E017. Chronic obstipation (constipation)
E018. Colon irritabile
E019. Diverticulitis
E020. Acquired lactose intolerance (lactose malabsorption)
E021. Fructose malabsorption
E022. Glutensensitive enteropathy (celiac disease)
E023. Colectomy
E024. Short Bowel Syndrome

Gastrointestinal tract - liver, gallbladder, bile ducts
E025. Acute and chronic hepatitis (inflammation of the liver)
E026. Cholelithiasis (bile stones)
E027. fatty liver
E028. cirrhosis

Gastrointestinal tract - Stomach and duodenal intestine
E029. Acute gastritis
E030. Chronic gastritis
E031. Stomach bleeding
E032. Ulcus ventriculi and duodenal ulcer
E033. Condition after gastric surgery

Gastrointestinal tract - oral cavity and esophagus
E034. Stomatitis
E035. Esophageal carcinoma (esophageal cancer)
E036. Refluosophagitis (heartburn)

Special diseases
E037. Phenylketonuria (PKU)
E038. Rheumatic joint diseases

Metabolism
E039. Obesity (overweight)
E040. Diabetes mellitus
E041. Eating disorders (underweight)

Fat metabolism
E042. Hypercholesterolaemia (increased cholesterol level)
E043. Hepatic Encephalopathy

Heart and circulation
E044. Arteriosclerosis (arterial calcification)
E045. Heart insufficiency
E046. Hypertension
E047. Hyperuricaemia and gout

Changed nutrient requirements
E048. In case of fever
E049. For malignant diseases
E050. After burns
E051. Radiation and chemotherapy

CANCER
E100. Pancreatic cancer
E101. Bladder cancer
E102. Blood cancer (leukemia)
E103. Breast cancer
E104. Colorectal cancer
E105. Gastric cancer
E106. Kidney cancer
E107. Esophageal cancer

TCM
E200. Bladder - moisture heat in the bladder
E201. Bladder - moisture and cold in the bladder
E202. Bladder - emptiness and cold in the bladder
E203. Large intestine - external cold affects the large intestine
E204. Large intestine - moisture heat in the large intestine
E205. Large intestine - heat blocks the intestine II acute
E206. Large intestine - dryness of the colon
E207. Large intestine - Yang deficiency (cold)
E208. Heart - Blood insufficiency
E209. Heart - Blood stagnation
E210. Heart - Fire
E211. Heart - Hot mucus clogs the heart pores

E212. Heart - Cold mucus clogs the heart pores
E213. Heart - Qi deficiency
E214. Heart - Yang deficiency
E215. Heart - Yin deficiency
E216. Liver - Ascending Liver Yang
E217. Liver - Blood deficiency
E218. Liver - Blood stagnation
E219. Liver - Moisture heat in liver and gall bladder
E220. Liver - Fire
E221. Liver - Gall bladder Qi-Empty
E222. Liver - Cold in the liver meridian
E223. Liver - Qi stagnation
E224. Liver - Wind
E225. Liver - Wind with ascending liver Yang
E226. Liver - Wind with blood anemic
E227. Liver - Wind with extreme heat
E228. Lung - Qi deficiency
E229. Lung - Mucus-moisture in the lungs
E230. Lung - Mucus-heat in the lungs
E231. Lung - Mucus-cold in the lungs
E232. Lung - Dryness of the lungs
E233. Lung - Wind-heat attacks the lungs
E234. Lung - Wind-cold affects the lungs
E235. Lung - Yin deficiency
E236. Stomach - Bloodstagnation
E237. Stomach - Fire
E238. Stomach - Cold with liquid
E239. Stomach - Nutrition stagnation
E240. Stomach - Qi deficiency
E241. Stomach - Rebellious Qi
E242. Stomach - Yin Emptiness
E243. Spleen - Heat and moisture attack the spleen
E244. Spleen - Coldness and moisture affects the spleen
E245. Spleen - Qi deficiency
E246. Spleen - Qi deficiency + Declining spleen Qi
E247. Spleen - Qi deficiency + spleen does not control the blood
E248. Spleen - Yang deficiency
E249. Kidney - Heart and kidney no longer communicate
E250. Kidney - Jing deficiency
E251. Kidney - Kidneys cannot receive the Qi
E252. Kidney - Qi is not stable
E253. Kidney - Yang deficiency
E254. Kidney - Yin deficiency

For further information visit di-book.com.